This Is What
I Want to Be

Zookeeper

Heather Miller

Heinemann Library
Chicago, Illinois

©2003 Reed Educational & Professional Publishing
Published by Heinemann Library,
an imprint of Reed Educational & Professional Publishing
Chicago, IL

Customer Service 888-454-2279
Visit our website at www.heinemannlibrary.com

Designed by Sue Emerson, Heinemann Library
Printed and bound in the United States by Lake Book Manufacturing, Inc.

07 06 05 04 03
10 9 8 7 6 5 4 3 2 1

Library of Congress Cataloging-in-Publication Data
Miller, Heather.
    Zookeeper / Heather Miller.
        p. cm. — (This is what I want to be)
Includes index.
Contents: What do zookeepers do? — What is a zookeeper's day like? —What do zookeepers wear? — What tools do zookeepers use? — Where do zookeepers work? — When do zookeepers work? — Do zookeepers work in other places? — What kinds of zookeepers are there? — How do people become zookeepers?
    ISBN: 1-4034-0373-2 (HC), 1-4034-0595-6 (Pbk.)
    1. Zoo keepers—Vocational guidance—Juvenile literature. [1. Zookeepers. 2. Occupations.] I. Title.
    QL50.5 .M56 2002
    636.088'9—dc21

                                        2001008140

Acknowledgments
The author and publishers are grateful to the following for permission to reproduce copyright material:
pp. 4, 11, 14 Phil Martin/Heinemann Library; pp. 5, 7, 13, 17 Jim Schulz/Chicago Zoological Society/The Brookfield Zoo; p. 6 Richard T. Nowitz/Photo Researchers, Inc.; pp. 8, 9, 10 D. Demello/Wildlife Conservation Society; p. 12 David Gray/Reuters; p. 15 AP Photo/Gary Green/Akron Beacon Journal; p. 16 Robert Brenner/PhotoEdit, Inc.; p. 18 W. Bertsch/Bruce Coleman Inc.; p. 19 Bob Daemmrich/Stock Boston; p. 20 Erwin C. Nielson/Mira.com; p. 21 Kimberly Barth/Akron Beacon Journal/KRT; p. 23 (row 1, L-R) D. Demello/Wildlife Conservation Society, Bob Daemmrich/Stock Boston, The Brookfield Zoo; p. 23 (row 2, L-R) Gregg Ozzo/Visuals Unlimited, W.Bertsch/Bruce Coleman Inc., Siede Preis/PhotoDisc; p.23 (row 3, L-R) PhotoDisc, D. Demello/Wildlife Conservation Society, Phil Martin/Heinemann Library; p. 23 (row 4, L-R) Jim Schulz/Chicago Zoological Society/The Brookfield Zoo, D. Demello/Wildlife Conservation Society

Cover photograph by Robert Brenner/PhotoEdit, Inc.
Photo research by Scott Braut

Every effort has been made to contact copyright holders of any material reproduced in this book. Any omissions will be rectified in subsequent printings if notice is given to the publisher.

Special thanks to our advisory panel for their help in the preparation of this book:

Eileen Day, Preschool Teacher
Chicago, IL

Ellen Dolmetsch, MLS
Wilmington, DE

Kathleen Gilbert,
Second Grade Teacher
Austin, TX

Sandra Gilbert,
Library Media Specialist
Houston, TX

Angela Leeper,
Educational Consultant
North Carolina Department
of Public Instruction

Raleigh, NC

Pam McDonald, Reading Teacher
Winter Springs, FL

Melinda Murphy,
Library Media Specialist
Houston, TX

The publishers would also like to thank Lee Haines, Assistant Director of Marketing and Public Relations at the Brookfield Zoo in Brookfield, Illinois, for his help in reviewing this book for accuracy and Jim Schulz, Brookfield Zoo's Staff Photographer, for his help in providing photos.

Some words are shown in bold, **like this.**
You can find them in the picture glossary on page 23.

Contents

What Do Zookeepers Do?

Zookeepers care for animals at the zoo.

They make sure each animal is healthy.

Zookeepers talk to visitors
about animals.

They help people learn about animals,
like this **guinea pig.**

What Is a Zookeeper's Day Like?

Zookeepers plan healthy meals for the animals.

They get food ready for each animal.

Zookeepers clean the animal **enclosures.**

They make it easier for the animals to keep clean.

What Do Zookeepers Wear?

Zookeepers wear **uniforms**.

Zookeepers sometimes wear tall
rubber boots.

They wear **masks** to keep germs away.

What Tools Do Zookeepers Use?

Zookeepers use **squeegees** to clean windows.

They spray water with **hoses**.

Zookeepers carry food to the animals in **wheelbarrows.**

Where Do Zookeepers Work?

Zookeepers work in the animals' enclosures.

Some zookeepers work in
the **nursery**.

They take care of baby animals.

Do Zookeepers Work in Other Places?

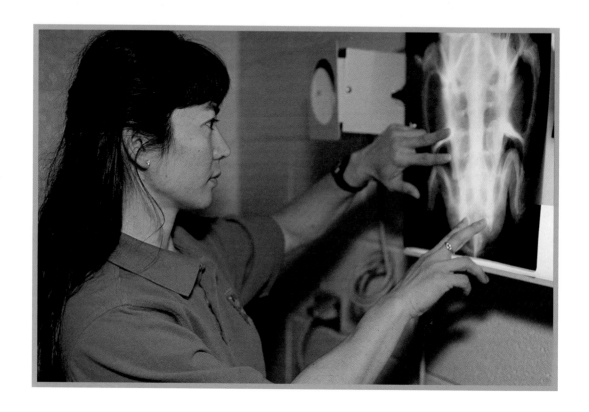

Some zoos have a special place for sick animals.

People who work there are called **zoo veterinarians.**

Zoo veterinarians give sick animals **medicine.**

When Do Zookeepers Work?

There are zookeepers at the zoo every day.

Animals need food and water every day.

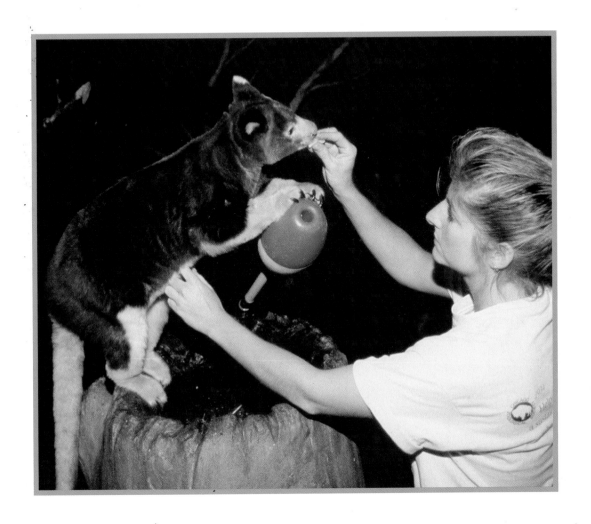

Night keepers work at night.

They check on the animals after
the zoo closes.

What Kinds of Zookeepers Are There?

Many zookeepers learn about one group of animals.

Reptile keepers take care of lizards and snakes.

Bird keepers care for birds.

This bird keeper feeds the **pelicans**.

How Do People Become Zookeepers?

People go to college to become zookeepers.

They learn about animals and science.

New zookeepers work with other zookeepers.

They learn how to care for many different animals.

Quiz

Can you remember what these things are called?

Look for the answers on page 24.

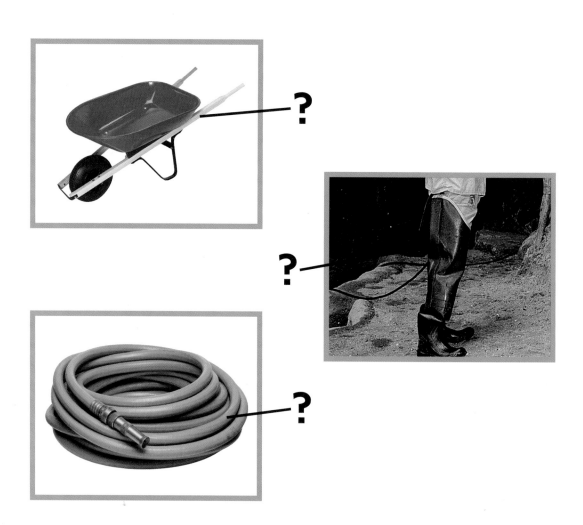

?

?

?

Picture Glossary

enclosure
pages 7, 12

medicine
page 15

reptile
page 18

uniform
page 8

guinea pig
page 5

nursery
page 13

rubber boots
page 9

wheelbarrow
page 11

hose
page 10

pelican
page 19

squeegee
page 10

zoo veterinarian
pages 14, 15

mask
page 9

23

Note to Parents and Teachers

Reading for information is an important part of a child's literacy development. Learning begins with a question about something. Help children think of themselves as investigators and researchers by encouraging their questions about the world around them. Each chapter in this book begins with a question. Read the question together. Look at the pictures. Talk about what you think the answer might be. Then read the text to find out if your predictions were correct. Think of other questions you could ask about the topic, and discuss where you might find the answers. Assist children in using the picture glossary and the index to practice new vocabulary and research skills.

Index

Answers to quiz on page 22

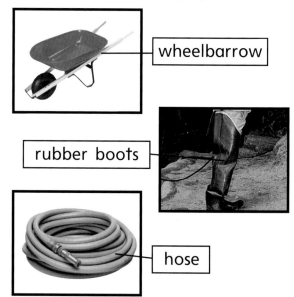

wheelbarrow

rubber boots

hose